I0622885

HOW TO PLAY HOUSE

BY HEATHER DORN

ROADSIDE PRESS

copy-right

How to Play House
Copyright © Heather Dorn 2023
ISBN: 979-8-9861093-4-3

All rights reserved. Printed in the United States of America. No part of this text may be used or reproduced in any manner without written permission from the author or publisher except in the case of brief quotations embodied in critical articles and reviews.

Editor: Michele McDannold
Cover Art: Aleathia Drehmer

Roadside Press
Meredosia, IL

CONTENTS

For my mother, who taught me that I could do anything.

I.

How To Cook in a Coffee Pot

Mom cleans the rooms so we can stay
rent free. Two beds, a bathroom, and a TV –
the Olympics are playing, which is
important to me. I never miss a chance to see
the tumbling girls, swimming women, running
stars who win gold medals. Some of them
younger than me and they already have a life
the whole world is watching.

Mom once said it was too late for me
that gymnasts are made as children
not teens. I could do other things instead.
Still, I practice balancing on the concrete wall
that divides the Motel from the grocery.
I walk-leap-walk and kick, then spin without falling
into the parking lot (automatic deduction)
and finally dismount, hands to the sky in victory.

Mom will wonder where I am if I'm late
getting in and I'm sure everyone wants
to eat, so I go home when the sky turns
streaked. And when I walk in, the coffee
pot is already on. It's filling with water
as the crushed ramen noodles spin past
one another, competing for space in their
cramped chamber. But ramen are used to this.

I sit next to my brother on our bed.
We are putting peanut butter on bread. I remember
when we had a fridge and ate
butter. Peanut butter and butter was almost
as good as Kraft macaroni and cheese. And I wonder
if mom could boil noodles in our coffee pot

and if we could use powdered milk (and skip
the butter) if it would taste at all the same

as the dinner I loved. When Hurricane Gilbert came
we had to move across the street to another motel
that didn't want a maid. Mom got a hot plate and
cooked sandwiches and we weren't to watch TV
all day anymore. So I practiced twirling around
the stairs, jumping into the air like a gymnast on uneven bars.
And as the wind picked up, I felt myself grow lighter
until eventually I could lift my body into the sky in victory.

HOW TO BUY GROCERIES

We sometimes didn't have any space
for storing them – our groceries
had to go with us to the park, motel,
next town in the middle of the night.
Crackers, peanut butter, that same can
of yams set on a new shelf. This is

natural. After the divorce
we stayed with my aunt while
mom was at the casinos: bread
green beans, corn, cheese, cereal
juice, hamburger. We ate
spaghetti like at home before

and milk with dinner, meat for lunch
on the weekend. But then we moved
out and around and sometimes into locked-door
apartments where we stayed as mom danced her crazy out
at nightclubs. She stumbled home
hoarding frozen taquitos. In jr. high, I don't know

where she is or what is wrong with me
when the blood comes. Our fridge is broken
and her beer crowds the only cool area
of the freezer. I wrap toilet paper I stole from church
around my panties. I mix powdered milk and
microwave cream corn from the food

basket the church gave us. In high school
mom leaves me $20 and goes to Mexico for
a week. She leaves a note that a check is coming

4.

and I can cash it, but I don't know where
a bank is or how to drive. I pour cereal,
mix water with powdered milk.

How To Name Your Daughter

My father called me *Heatherino, my little bambino.* He let me sit below the couch he slept on. He let me sit in the bathroom crying while he pretended to get a screwdriver he already had. He never saw me sit on the stairs while he beat mom into a ball on that brown chair.

My grandfather called me *Feather.* He had a bad ticker and a worse sense of humor that I got too. His joke was, "Eat every bean and pea on your plate." He couldn't let go of newspapers and I look at my stack of student portfolios hogging the closet. He had heart attacks, but I only got the pacemaker.

My father called me *Bitch* the last time I heard his voice. I was 10. I wanted to go to camp and it cost money and we had none. Mom said to ask him, so I did. *You're just like your mother*, he also said.

I wanted my name to be Ginger. Like in *Gilligan's Island.* I wanted to be treated like someone important and for my hair to flip out red and to be sexy so people would pay attention to me and I could never be invisible.

When I got older, I told everyone on playground that I was the real Punky Brewster. And that I had to remain anonymous. And that the people I lived with were not my parents but a secret FBI family. Everything but my fame was Top Secret. The next day, everybody was laughing at me. I wanted to be Ginger again, but shipwrecked and alone.

My mother called me, *Pretty* and we trolled businesses for sponsors. *Will you give my daughter money to be in a pageant? Can you offer a dress?* After the pageant the modeling agent pinched my leg, *You're too short; try acting with those thighs.*

I remember jumping in a hotel pool for five takes. Then years of high school theatre competition. In a one-act play I was the Queen of Troy after the war. The lights lowered, I spoke and people hushed. I could make people cry. I liked doing it.

My mentor called me *talented*, reading my crappy poetry. Said he imagined that my gift had come as some consolation for my childhood. I thought back to sleeping in our van. I thought back to thinking, *This must be what a stakeout is like.* Thinking, *I wish we had a refrigerator.* I laughed to end the conversation, like a girl at a bar laughs at a man her dad's age. I laughed because I could only speak on a page. I sat on his couch for years. He taught me to watch my self. Taught me what my writing did so I could control it. The way a line can hang

or keep going and the tone that could create. He called my tone menacing and my voice a little girl, he guessed about 10. His voice was still 12. Once I knew she was there, I could let her grow up. He taught me teaching is love first, never *us vs. them.* Said to write a draft for yourself where the step-dad gets whatever he gets. Revise it reasonably. Then back through again. He taught me how to be a tattletale and not a victim. He taught me to turn the knife on a page.

Mom once said that she named me after a famous soap opera character of the time. She said, *She was a murderer and so beautiful.* I understood her expectations.

Now when she calls me, I can smell the cheap vodka through my cell phone. She repeats stories. Recounts purchases. Gossips about people I don't know. Repeats stories; words loose. I tell her I need to go 16 times.

When the phone rings the next night, she expects me to bounce quick and answer. I flip off the TV. The phone keeps ringing and

I grab my pen. It rings again.
I open my journal.

It rings and rings. I click off the sound to my phone and swipe at her face so it goes away to darkness. In my mind, it goes away to nothingness to a black hole of loss. I write my story. I sign my name in every line.

Ballerinas Don't Eat Cheezits

There's a clock as tall as my father
that tells me what time it's supposed
to be. The pendulum falls like a drip
and ticks right and left and right.

Sometimes my stair steps trip me
and my legs tumble like laundry clothes
until I hit the hat rack by the front door.

I once asked for a toy in the grocery
after being told not to ask for a toy
in the grocery. I went straight home
to my room, no ice cream. I felt the loss
as one would any close friend.

There is a snake who looks scary
but isn't. He twists his
life around my own. We go to the fences
behind the apartment buildings
where the trains rattle through
and I push my snake in the boy's faces
until they scream for me to stop.
I'm mad that they put grease on my leg.

From the upstairs room where I sleep
I once watched my father come home and I waved
not remembering it was past my bedtime
not remembering I was meant to be lying
down. Mr. Roboto had come on the radio. I danced
six and forgetful. He roared up the stairs
shook me back to bed.

The earthquakes shake everything loose:

pictures, pans, Atari controllers,
hair, sweat, Pepsi bottles. They are bound
to break. And I am bound to step on them.

I get stuck in the bathroom and the tile floor feels
like icy pops and I'm crying because my father says
he doesn't know if he can get me out, and he knows
he can't fit macaroni and cheese under the door.

I sit at the top of the stairs and hear dad snap mom into the
chair,

I hear her cry and fire from his mouth and she apologizes
for being. She pretends she never shook.
She pretends concealer fixes the marriage.

My mother drew us while we played
in the living room floor. I was eager to see the way
she formed my lines, how she made my shape.

My father was asleep.

My brother decided he wanted to have his way
and if he couldn't that he would bang his head
into the ground until he passed out
or bled. My mother held his head
for hours.

The earthquakes shake everything loose:
phone numbers, forgotten birthdays, *fishing is for boys* dad
says and *go do something with art instead.*

Ballerinas don't eat cheezits dad said and so I put them away for a week. Or it may have been an hour. I put the idea of dancing in my bottom drawer, with fashion model. Flat. The pendulum drips and dad tells me to sit up straight,

I'm more attractive that way.

How To Make Ends Meet

I used to think the saying went:
"How to make ends meat," like
something you'd throw in a stew
because if you worked hard enough
you could scrape together enough
to buy beef parts or the legs of chickens.
These were the ends of the meat.

I felt a little bad for the snap-necked
chickens and I felt like She-Ra
with the power of Grayskull and protein
inside me. I didn't even like meat
that much, it was tough to chew
and inconsistent as my mother's men.
But our once-a-week meat night
was a window to the dream, so we

had to finish all our meat before we could
eat bread. I remember thinking
about my mom working hard for the dentist,
staying late to scrub teeth
and then also cleaning homes on the side
(sometimes she was a night-time
bookkeeper). I remember a grisly piece
of meat sticking in my teeth wishing she
hadn't wasted her nights for this –

that if we couldn't have front meat
what was the point in trying?

How To Manage

My mother had a job
as the manager of a 7-11.

She made big changes: Hot dogs to be thrown
every two hours, no more week-long

hot chocolate, the machines were all cleaned
daily, the books in order, the floor mopped.

My brother and I came to work and played
in the back office or laid at the video store

watching cartoons on the TVs, with fresh
hot dogs and cocoa. She was never done

because people couldn't come in or forgot
or the store was just robbed and everybody else

was too scared. So mom went down there
alone.

I didn't go that day. Mom never asked.
I didn't go. Stayed with my stepdad

alone. A different kind
of threat.

I.   I Don't Remember
- A.   The time my dad held my mother unlike a ragdoll.
  - a.   unlike a tambourine.
  - b.   unlike an earthquake.
- B.   The time he took me fishing even though I was a girl.
- C.   The time he was sober.
- D.   The time my mother put on eye makeup just to look pretty.
  - a.   just on the top of her eyes.
- E.   The time my mother married a man who was gentle.
- F.   The time I talked back against the rumors that my brother was crazy.
  - a.   and I believed he was sane.
- G.   The time I hugged him.
- H.   The time I loved my body.
  - a.   looked at my stomach
  - b.   accepted a compliment
  - c.   wanted my clothes off.
- I.   The time I didn't pass a mirror and search for flaws in my nose or teeth.
- J.   The time my report card was good enough.
  - a.   A
  - b.   A
  - c.   A
  - d.   doesn't matter.
- K.   The time I was full.
- L.   The time I believed I was sane.
  - a.   and I believed it.
  - b.   and I believed it.

II.   I Remember

Everything is like fireworks at the apartments and there is gravel in my feet and I feel like I'm being shaken to rattle by the train who carries important things to important people while the boys in the apartments smear grease on my leg and call me a sissy.

I convince my brother to swap me a nickel for his dime. *Mine's bigger. Don't you want the bigger coin,* I say. Soon, he will throw desks at teachers. Beaten by our dad and then preachers, he will be put in the mental hospital. They will make him drool with meds. *Say no to drugs,* except these. He will exchange Nintendo games for weed when he gets out. These are his best decision.

Everything is like a firework inside me and I can't stand any part of me. If I can explode myself I'll feel more worthy of being matter. My mouth's too big for its own good and I'm a smart ass and it'll get me in trouble one day, the he's all said. And then he grabbed the back of my head and mashed it in his palm like an egg and my knees buckled, ready to crack.

D.A.R.E.

I already knew some of the drugs. By fifth grade,
my mom had grown skunk plants in you-must-not-
open-closet. My brother cut his foot on the mirror
with the white snow. He shouldn't
have crawled under the bed. The work

sheet showed a list of ways to influence
someone to do drugs. Next to "Bandwagon"
a group of kids drawn on a hay ride saying
"Everyone's doing it!" I thought they seemed
happy, too happy to be bad guys, but they

were bad the officer said. He was not
tolerant of excessive happiness. I remember
looking at his gun. That was another technique
of persuasion. I studied these methods
of influence, eager to see how I might manipulate

words to do what I wanted. The officer announced
there was an essay contest. The winner would
read at graduation. So I wrote about how bad
drugs were and how I would never do them. I said
other kids should join me. That it's dumb to do drugs

and I listed famous people who thought so too.
I found quotes and made grand claims. I didn't believe
what I was writing, but I didn't believe
anything else either. Mom couldn't come to see me
read. She was scrubbing

someone's teeth at the time, but she would have
enjoyed the end when I called for a revolution.

When I got home, I sat on the couch and read her the paper. I watched her smoke a blunt and hoped the school would never come and find us out.

How To Move

We move using big black garbage bags
tied loosely to the top of the car. We move
often, bags our only suitcase. In 5th grade

a bag came undone
as we were driving down some un-known
highway, spilling our few luxuries
past the broken   white lines

one of my Garfield slippers resting
in road-side rocks. Even in an emergency
he was so lazy. And my step-dad says

we can't go back. A textbook is in my
backpack by my feet. The school told us
to bring those back and I feel horrible
for stealing it. I can't look at the pages
because of guilt and car sickness.

Everything is sacrificed to the highway.
Inside the cars and out. A sneaker tumbles
in the gravel, trying to get home.

I've heard that shoes become
like their owners. A book sits on a bench
in the rain. A crumpled bumper lies in the grass
like a pin up model
curving toward and away from
her own body.

Rituals

III.

I live in the spare room in my fiancé's parents' house. I put my shampoo and conditioner in the bathtub next to his. Every day when I get in to take a shower, it has been buried in the back of the cabinet again.

shampoo slathers slick
bubbles smell like strawberries
and burning bridges

II.

I wish I could have folded my body into my junior high gym locker. I wish I could have made myself some secret escape to the field of flowers. I wish the shorts had been longer than a dollar bill's width and that the man-coach would have stood at our heads.

wait for the late bell
water only feels good when
nobody's watching

I.

We sleep in an apartment that is burned on the inside, the living room like toast, every smell choking me so I spend every day outside and only come inside at night to share a charred bed, our own blanket beneath us, torn in the most familiar ways, silky borders ripped like a hiding place.

mother turned the knob
let the remaining water
baptize me in ash

THE THINGS I DON'T KNOW

How to tell time with no lines on the clock.
How fractions work. Where the fork
and spoons go. Popular music from my
graduating year.

How to make lasagna. How to sew a sweater.
How to fix a car. How to inflate a tire.
How to cut a 2x4. How to go to bed at night.
How to follow instructions.

The names of more than ten cheeses. Wine pairings
for meat or vegetables. What that fruit is.
What escargot tastes like. Latin.
The names of the fast piano songs I prefer.

How to play an instrument. How to pronounce: *diegesis*.
How catnip makes my best friend bite me. Why I still reach
for him. Why the sound of heavy feet walking up stairs
makes my neck shiver. Where I go when I stop talking

and then start a minute later. Why it feels strange
to admit disassociation. My elementary school teachers'
names. How many times we moved. How many schools
I went to. How many books I begged to return

to the schools I suddenly left. How to make friends.
How to fight without yelling. How to love without fighting.
How to stop hating my father for his presence, for his
absence. Where my mother went when she was gone.

How many times my step-dad came into my dark room.
Where my mother was. How many cans of vegetables
we had for the weekend. Where my mother was. How to fix
a broken fridge. Where my mother was.

Bugs on a Window in Arkansas

His fingers are fast like notes plinked too hard on a piano
and I can see trees I know well out the window and I think of
climbing higher than the branches to where clouds touch

music. I close my eyes and hear nothing
on purpose. My room is dark and I become asleep
on purpose and my mind is tabula rasa. Then I'm a

famous artist (see the turtle I drew and sent in
with the brochure). I'm good at Garfield too. I'm a
fashion doll, who is still and turned and played

with the best night gowns, the best make-up
and hair. I can stare at nothing like the backs of my eyes.
I'm a mermaid if I can hear the sea in a rainstorm.

I can go to where water washes wounds open.
I'm faster than a dolphin. I can hold my breath
for a year. After he came in my room I decide he

didn't. All I remember is being a still doll,
weighted lids tipped down. All I remember
is bugs in my nightgown. All I remember

is a blank page. All I remember
is closed eyes. All I remember
is nothing.

FERAL

My mother almost always had a job
and when I knew my father
he was stuck on a jobless couch not looking,
drinking beer and waiting
for my mother to cook dinner. My brother

screeched when he got mad and banged his head
into the floor until he bled. He scared me
like maybe the earthquake we had when mom was pregnant
shook him crazy. Like maybe he was everything
of my father alone.

My father came home drinking and shook
my mother. My father came home from having fun
mad. He didn't like the dinner she'd saved. He thought she'd
cook it later when it was closer to midnight than
five. I sat at the top of the stairs until he was done

with her. I sat at the top of the stairs alone until
one day we left him.

I didn't want to see my stepfathers so I hid
in my room.

My stepfathers and mom went away for days and I would
make a sandwich. Canned vegetables.
Powdered milk. I fed the scraps to my brother like he was
a dog. One day when I was 13, he found a bee in his room
and cried for me to save him from it.
I shut and locked my door, and put clothes
under the crack so the bee couldn't weave in and sting me.

I read books in my room, in my closet,
about high school girls with pig's blood dumped on them.
I think this will be me. I read about Helen
being a friend to Jane and think, *this will never be me.*
I read about Pip and think, *I would be very suspicious.*
I think I know Estella. A boy who I won't date says she is me
but I think she is the girl who sits next to me
in Anatomy with the huge blue eyes.

I took to eating nothing but peas for a month as a teen.
We had cans of peas and corn
and sometimes green beans

and sometimes bread or cheese.
Ration the good food or you must
eat the big can of yams we've had since forever.
Nobody knows where it came from
but there are no marshmallows
or brown sugar or other forms of sugar.

When I was in high school I tried to make cookies
with a friend, while my stepfather and mother
were in Mexico. We mixed up flour and water
and I couldn't think of anything else to add
so I baked them on high. When I tasted the result:
burnt clumps of dense dough,
I realized how little I had learned.

THESE ARE THE THINGS I LEARNED FROM MY MOTHER

Lipstick doubles
as blush
midnight is the best
time to vacuum
looks matter more
than your pre-school
teacher will admit

nobody will get your drink
for you
men like to
be right
sometimes
your best
isn't good enough

LIBRARIES & MUSEUMS

I sit on orange carpet in the valleys
between the tall stacks of books.
Cheeto orange floor, staining
memories like sun on an old photo.

The journals next to me are *M*'s:
Manuals & handbooks

The smell like a collection of newspapers
my grandpa kept stacked to the ceiling,
a whole room in his house.

Mergers & acquisitions.

While grandma weighed bran flakes,
he ate the okra she fried us. The okra
he grew us. She cleaned up and grandpa
made cartoon art out of stamps – Popeye
was my favorite. I wondered if he sent
all those letters to get all those stamps.
Who did he send them to?

Memory & cognition.

We went to *The Greasy Spoon*
and I watched grandpa
have a heart attack
in a diner booth
next to me. *The Greasy Spoon*
he called it when we came in.
I watched my mother
yell for 911, do CPR.
I watched the free ice cream
dribble down his cheek. Free.

Late Fines

I'm on the highway again
in the same van
going to
nobody knows yet,
maybe Arkansas.

I'm wanting
to be tied to a tree
or a post or an idea.

I'm wanting
to return my overdue library books
that I thought I'd have time to return
before we tied our clothes
in trash bags again
and left again to
not sure now,
maybe Missouri,
though step-dad likes Vegas.

I'm looking out the car window
at how trees pass by
like news in a microfiche machine.
I'm looking at left-to-right flight
across the page sky.

I'm watching for my mother
moon who never leaves forever.
I'm waiting for her
to find me through the clouds
wherever our car drives
and I wish that I could tie a string
to her and me,

like doors to stubborn teeth
not ready to leave, so she could always
find me. And I'm hoping
next time I will know when
to turn my books in
and what
to burn to my skin.

How To Play Barbie

You be the army man we stole from my brother's room
and I'll be my Barbie. My Barbie's name
is Ginger. You can swing by the dream house at eight –
tour the 10 rooms, finished attic, swing set.
You can say my high heels drive you
wild when you pull up for our date in some
car that makes as much noise as the cheap, broke ones
but with less smoke.

I will build the dream house while you're gone:
use kitchen drawers for rooms
use the pizza box cheese guards as end tables
tie sandwich baggies as waterbeds
a push-up-pop for a parasol and if I can
convince mom the hole is accidental, a sock could become
a new dress with a pink stripe around the bottom.
I will snip it just short enough to get on the cover of *Seventeen*.
I can make it a blanket for the waterbed. At school
I stapled these paper throw pillows for the rag couch I'd rolled up,
hidden, under my sheets.

Pick me up and take me away to the t-shirt drawer. Bring
me home and put me on the holy sock waterbed. Bang
your body into me so the water will ripple. Say "I love you."
And then say you will come back for me when you're done
drinking with your friends. And my mother yells at me
for playing with water and using up a baggie and a rubber band and
for keeping a push-up pop parasol, stuck to the carpet now

and my father yells at my mother for everything else and he repaints it
all on her face so she will
never forget and my army men leave
out the back door behind my father

28.

and I watch all the men walk away, while others
take their place – the next one visible
always another marching in
even now.

CRAWDADS

I ate crawdads my only Pennsylvania summer
two months a step-daughter, cartwheeling
on grass without sticker burrs, somersaults

no longer hurt and pizza was a dollar a slice.
I slept on the floor of my step-sister's room
and tried to sneak her fashion dolls when she

was away at college. My step-brother taught me
how to catch lunch in the neighbor's creek. We
stood in the stream, one foot on the shore, ready

to run in case of injury or tattletales. My mother
cooked what we brought home. She didn't know
we were poachers. It was don't ask, don't tell.

She made dinner a project, like something I might
get an *A* for. My new step-dad liked crawdads too,
encouraged us to catch them. He drank beer

then tore their heads off. He drank whisky after that.
I ate crawdads after I watched my mother murder them
drop them in the boil, lipstick red and screaming.

Sometimes when my step-dad drank too much, he found
his war memories and gunbox. One day I hid
with the other kids in my step-brother's bedroom

door locked, until we crawled out the window past shrubs
to a neighbor's waiting van. I slept with her daughters –
clowns and crosses on the wall – four sister wives, blankets

piled on us like shields, teddy bears our Christian husbands.
I borrowed a t-shirt that was too big so I could be modest
on a night so hot, it must have been angry too.

The fan spun deliberately, so as to make good decisions.
The next day, mom took us back to the step-dad and all summer
I caught crawdads, stole my step-sister's Darcy dolls,

kissed my step-brother on the bunk bed we hid under.

WE ARE THE PITY CHILDREN

We wear your company t-shirts as pajamas and sleep on your children's trundle beds when our mother swings at her new husband or he brings out his gun. We don't know the word trundle, but we've slept on enough pull out, shaky, extra mattresses to know it means stability. Our mattresses are usually on the floor, if we have them at all. We are the Pity Children and we have nothing if we have anything at all and that is how you like it so you can fill us up. You give us hairclips because we sit in your class with wild, dirty hair and do well on tests. You say you just can't use them, like giving them to us was an afterthought and we love you more for it. You give us tortillas every morning and a ride to school. You never say anything when we slather butter until it drips. Your daughter doesn't even like us and you give us a tortilla to make up for it and it does and we want her to hate us again for another tortilla. We are the Pity Children and you give us a food basket and a box of old clothes and a prayer and we are to *Thank you very much* and be *So so grateful* when we see you. And we are to mention it the second and third time too. And we are to be *So so grateful*.

MEN TEACH ME LOVE

When I was three
my father would tickle me
relentlessly, prodding
poking, every part of my stomach
and ribs as I begged
for him to stop
not wanting to feel
the tingling, touching
vulnerable pinches
screaming as I was punished
for being too loud.

When I was eight
my stepfather came
into my room
after bedtime
like it was his own
and I closed my eyes
until I was so far in the sky
I could only see stars
who flew far away from home
and planets too big
to be captured and held down.

When I was eleven
my teenage cousin
chased me around
the backyard saying
he was going to make out with me.
In the laundry room
he pinned my hands behind me
This is what adults do.

When I was thirteen
men from church would ask me
to date their brothers, cousins,
sometimes friends.
Gotta keep it in the family
one man said, planning to date me
when I turned eighteen.
I don't want to get arrested.

He thought it was a dumb law,
put his hands under my skirt
in the back of the church bus.
His cousin was going to hold his place
like a bookmark.

When I sit in bars now,
men tell me about my body.
Some men see a ring
and apologize
because they stepped on
some other man's
property – the SOLD sticker
not bold enough.

One man at a bar told me
he liked my eyes and he bet
I could sing pretty
if I stay not too drunk. I said
nothing, ignored him.
When he left I was gnawing
on a chicken wing
sauce all over my nose and mouth.
He walked past me,
put a stranger – hand
on my shoulder and said,
I had fun watching you tonight.

How To Be a Woman in a Man's Idea

I fall down the stairs like a rag doll
again and again when I'm four.
The hat rack breaks my body's tumble
and I thump to a stop. Nobody ever
moves that hat rack, maybe worried
I'd crack headfirst into the wall instead.
Better to be impaled. There is something

slippery about being four and next to the steps
in my house. There is something
that still pushes me over the edge
of that first step now. I have seen how
this is inherited. I watched my brother
bang his three year old head into concrete
over and over again. He is too

sturdy to fall down the stairs and has to
break himself another way instead. I see
my mother's face, like blue ink spilled
on her eyes. She did not fall, whatever
she says. I watch my father's fist raise
above her, gripped, as if he held the pen
that would ink her face. There is something

hopeful about being a woman in a man's
story. Step fathers like to stare and I learn
there is a violence that is quietly louder. There is
something that still pushes at the edges of
comfort when men talk to me. As if the switch
reads: "Medusa/ Kitten." There is something
about the way my father's lamb was not done right
and when people finally care about Janay Rice because they saw
the video, I remember how much like brushing my teeth it felt,
sitting at the top of the stairs, listening to my mother cry.

And I never knew when the step-he would come
into my dark room or bend my body
on the couch as I half-slept or grab the back
of my head in his palm, gathering the hair
like a twisted ponytail, pushing me lower.

I fall down like a doll, over and over, there is
something slippery about being a woman
in a man's idea. If he says *Hi,* I want
to tell him *fuck off!* But if he tells me
Watch where the hell you're going! my instinct

is to follow him home purring,
and beg to curl at his feet.
Wait til he's asleep, then
take a sharp, deep, slice at his throat
and crawl back street side.

IMPRINTING

I'm tiring of confinement – this place filling
of connections. They are spilling
on the deck and out the front door

to go smoke, they are cluttering
the booths and barstools, making it impossible to move.
Bartender knows my name

and my lungs begin to feel under water,
there are more than three of us at the table.
My friend tells a hilarious story

about a double date she and her boyfriend went on
with her sister and suddenly everyone has a story
about their sister or brother or not having one – hilarious

or cute, or they say *Don't you have a brother?*
I never went on a double date with my brother
never had a heart-to-heart about our feelings

or family or favorite food, we never had
inside jokes or outside
contact. I pretend to forget him

and he embarrassed me by remembering
my name in public because he had nothing to lose
and he wanted half of my good fortune and to see me crash.

They continue their stories and it is not just brothers
and sisters. It is mothers who hum Baby Got Back
while they clean, it is fathers who shave their legs on a dare,

it is cousins who failed math twice but teach math now
and grandparents who repeat stories
about the day they met Gordie Howe.

For them, life has been a web of connections
for me, life has been a collection of sensory neurons.
They have been hugged, gathered, and imprinted.

I have fallen down the stairs and hidden.
They say, *Don't you have a brother?*
and I remember the fire he almost started

the church he broke into, remember the way we fought
over food and the radio – not yelling, screaming
and sent to time out, but a punch to the nose

or boot to the mouth and there's nobody to tell but
nobody. I still see the scar from where he burned me
with the curling iron. I'd reminded him

he was *a stupid dick* and he disagreed. I still see him
sitting in the mental hospital with drool slipping
from his lips.

That was the closest I've ever felt to him.

I say this with a long silence
to their question.

Sometimes they complain
about their families, the extended
relatives that annoy,

or the mother who insists on a nightly text.
Growing up, they felt drowned
in entanglements

and I felt suffocated by open air.

13 Ways of Looking at My Mother

I.
I see her prancing
in circles with the dog
drunk and happy
her hair like a daisy
windmill around her face.

II.
She makes Kraft
macaroni with yogurt
for creaminess.

III.
In the winter she shrivels
into a ball on the couch
and watches *The Closer.*

IV.
In the mirror, when I am pregnant
with my second child,
I see her grey eyes
staring at me.

V.
A memory
of her
drawing my face.

VI.
The cats always peed
in her Jeep.

VII.
My father's fist
on her face. She tried
not to cry.

VIII.
She wears a toothbrush
necklace. She believes hygiene
is important.

IX.
She gets marriage proposals
on the second date. Most of the time
she turns them down.

X.
She stopped smoking. Again.

XI.
She yells at me for never answering
my phone when I answer
her calls.

XII.
She says
I am perfect.

XIII.
She wants to know if
I've lost weight.

Selfie #4

The woman in the commercial
can finally talk
to her daughter who lives ten
states away. They cry
on the line over how their connection
is so clear. I'm in bed, my pj's
spaghettio-stained and ready for
the washer. 12 missed calls
I let myself miss another.
I'm in bed crying
for their connection
and clear conversation. I straighten my
tiara, try to stop
tearing because the phone won't stop
ringing, face smeared
with blots of mascara and red wine.

How To Compete

She has limp hair and she sounds dumb,
you said, mothering in the way you knew how,
giving me tips as a girl on beauty
pageants and being a woman. We watched

Miss Tennessee take the stage, sparkle
dress pooling around her feet like a lake
of diamonds. Miss Tennessee had never
chewed with her teeth or had coffee. It's risky,

staining yourself that way. Miss Tennessee
had been kissed by the sun and that suited her
skin, which had to be tabula rasa. It's why
nobody had tattoos or piercings or opinions.

It's why you told me not to get a tongue ring
You'll break a tooth! you said *And anyway
nobody will want to sponsor you then.*
Do you remember going from the dry cleaners

to the ice cream shop asking for money for pageants?
Do you remember turning me to the left
and then to the right, like a melon at the market,
to show them I was almost ripe? *This is the walk*, you said

and did the walk, swaying your hips, while we
yelled for someone on tv to lose, fumbling
over shoes, tripping on her dress. You showed me
success can be someone else's failure.

Some mornings while I get ready for work
I can hear you in my head while I look in the mirror,

She has limp hair and she sounds dumb. I scrunch my hair
up with water, look at my lip ring you don't like.

You send me too small clothes and ask if I've lost
weight. Text dozens of pictures of yourself
in bikinis and half shirts. I remember my first Thanksgiving
married, you opened the door to your apartment,

Crown-Royal-drunk. You didn't wear underwear
sat down next to my husband, since yours had just left.
You slurred something about potatoes, opened your legs.
You knew success could be someone else's failure.

How to Grow Up With Good Teeth

My mother hid under her bed
at thirteen, when the dried blood
moon came to occupy the sky, knowing this
was Judgment

her father struck her for coming home
with her shirt inside out
a mistake, after swimming in her big sister's
apartment pool, a mistake

my father on the couch, drinking
my mother's face bruised
a day after nobody is punching
and yelling, when she might feel safe
to stop and have a Pepsi, a drink she offers
one gulp each
the last Pepsi
sticky with our prints

she looks at my report card, says, *You can do it*
I know you can do it, and you could do better

she complained to the school
when I got blamed for something I didn't do
when the principal was threatening to spank me
for talking too much at lunch,
        in my memory, she roared through the doors
threw some *fucks* and *lawyers* at him
and we stormed out
but my memory was young and partial to soap operas

my step-dad swinging for my mother's face
or the dark glasses she wore for a week after

and they were all the same
men, they were
possessive and jealous and showy and angry and shallow and
mean they were him –

the grandfather I loved
who hit my mother first

the father I loved
who hit my mother next
while we watched
TVs with wire hangers for hair
we ate bread with butter when we
could afford it and milk with dinner
and brushes for our teeth
from mom's dental assisting job

all this until at least six years old
and sometimes after

and a Teddy Ruxpin once
and a Cabbage Patch because of a connection
a Get in Shape Girl rhythmic ribbon
and sometimes house change for Wintergreen Tic-Tacs
and Archie comic books

she knew how to make me look
threw my denim in the wash with bleach so I could have
acid washed jeans, took me to the thrift store
for prom dresses – limited selection
but get one with a rip that we can haggle and fix

everything is temporary

everything is negotiable.

How To Commit Suicide

When my mom gets drunk
she calls me crying about how mean
her husband is being. She wants my husband
to call her husband and make him stop.

She accuses me of not picking up my phone.
When my mother is drunk she says I don't post
enough status updates about her on Facebook.
She asks me how much weight I've gained

and if I'll quit my medication to lose it.
When my mom gets drunk she tells me
about my Uncle Pete, "I really think he killed
himself on purpose." The more she drinks

the more sure she is, "He was just depressed."
But she draws the word depressed out like a snake.
She wants to tell me the details and it sounds
like a recipe: "First he ate the codeine

then he mixed the crank in a spoon, then he shot
up under his tongue." She stops short of 'Finally
he died.' "I would never do crank," my mom says
shaking her pill bottle, pouring more vodka.

II.

Proofing

When I was eight, I did a report in school on the Egyptians
and I saw how smart they were to love cats. I decided
I wanted to be mummified when I died and I never

reconsidered. My college major was chosen by the shortest
registration line. Nobody wanted to be an English major
so it was perfect. Because I hated math. And didn't yet know

about sociology or archeology. Or psychology or law
or neurology or history. I didn't know that there was a t-shirt
that read: "I'm an English major, do you want fries with that?"

I outlined the Romantics by Roman Numerals. I. Blake
"A Poison Tree." II. Shelley "Ozymandias" III. Where
are the women? Where are the women? There's more Shelley's.

Now, I learned to read backwards. One letter at a time, then one
sentence. I learned to focus in on each spider's eye and see from
his perspective. Nobody cares about the fly's and I try to never waste

words. After I write suicide notes, I burn them. Except the one
I wrote in a mixed state and buried behind the garage. I wish
I could read it now to look for my mistakes.

Milk Carton Mother

My kids used to ask where I was going when I left home.
I'd say I was going to run away to China. Four year olds
think running away to China is funny. I never laughed.

I'd look at their round faces, fat like bakery cakes
with layers of frosting, so sweet
it puckered my soul. I'd feel their sticky fingers grasp

my legs and arms, face and hair, ears and mouth
their fingers invading my nose and blouse
while I was out in public. They'd let their bodies go limp

protesting sugar rations and make sounds like fire engines.
I never told them I was going to China during the wailing.
There's no time to go to China, or even think of it

when a toddler blocks traffic; there's no way to get a plane
ticket when the account has $7.73 left; I have to switch formula
again, each baby a different allergy.

When they fall asleep, their faces become doll faces
and I think they must be porcelain –
too precious to hold. If I book a flight
I could still not mess this up.

This is like syrup
too sweet to tolerate, too sticky to leave,
I feel swallowed up in it and stuck to the carpet.

This is when I plan my escape, in the middle of the night,
halos above their sleeping heads, I would sneak
through an open window with my backpack.

I would get on a bus, then a plane. I would meet some man
selling vacuum cleaners and wine. I wouldn't want either
but I'd take his card anyway so if I died, the police would have
some business card to trace me back to who I used to be.

Back home, I would be
a faded picture on the side of a milk carton:
"Have you seen this Woman-Child?"

My kids would pour my face
on nutritious oatmeal, not even recognizing
the woman who fed them her TV dinner carrots,
because they are mushy and probably
nutritious.

I'd visit temples and palaces and rivers and parks
and lakes and that huge Buddha statue.

I'd live like a spy, always ready to run
no pictures, no mail, no trace of a way for anyone
to grab or find me when I've decided I'm gone.

I'd live like a man, steel-toed boots, walking alone
at night.

I'd live like a cat, chasing moonbeams, sleeping
in sunbeams. Like a baby, unneeded. Like a boss, avoided.

But at home, when I walk toward the door to get groceries
or go to school or work

my kids cling to my clothes, body, hair and ask where
I'm going. "I'm going to run away to China," I say

straight-faced as they giggle and jump, crash
their bodies into mine, pulling themselves into my ribs
and stomach, pulling themselves toward my womb
like they are trying to be reborn.

A Royal Wave

The news alerts me:
Kate Middleton looks stunning
less than 10 hours after giving birth.

On tv she stands outside the hospital
smiling in a dress meant to pretend
post-birth bellies have no bumps
and uncurled hair is offensive to the nation:

How did she get that bounce?
an anchor woman wants to know,
touching her own locks,
How does she look so good so soon
after giving birth? I didn't look like that!

The newswoman is jealous and in awe.
She hates Kate Middleton for her bounce.
She loves Kate Middleton for her bounce.
Women online ask how to do it.

They have their hair tied in knots or wrapped
around a pencil, like me. They haven't sat down
all day, except to read that Kate Middleton
looks stunning still. Even if her dress doesn't

hide that she just had a baby.
It's the least the dress can do for the rest of us
because we don't celebrate our dresses stained spaghettio

pulled tight from multiple post-birth bellies, babies
who hang to our bodies so long they become
permanent weight, even when they move

to college. We don't celebrate frizzed hair pulled up
like an emergency. We celebrate the absence
of these things. The newswoman says,

She is a very careful woman.
She knows every step is being watched. She's been careful
to make sure every step is the right one.

Kate Middleton looks like a model.
She smiles. Her newborn is wrapped in a blanket
like my kids were when they were born.
She smiles and smiles and holds.

The newswoman asks,
How does she do everything right
everything perfectly?
she shakes her head

throws her hands up,
I feel completely inadequate.
Her male guest interrupts:
Well she's not an ordinary woman.

It's clear Kate Middleton
is the thing to be – that bounce, dress
face, smile, class, clothes, money.
Not this flat hair, dirty

for days, pajamas all week
$5 pizza dinner, children running
like dogs through the neighborhood
ordinary. The media is impressed.

She's an extraordinary woman
she never speaks to the press.

She hasn't said a word.

How does she get that bounce?
She's an extraordinary woman.
She never speaks.

Everyday Edna

All the mothers at the park
love their children so loud to each other
push them higher than college tuition. Smile
like they have won something, like you can win
by wiping the dirt from a face or sweeping a floor.
I wonder why I can't feel like Adele Ratignolle
in *The Awakening* – a mother – woman.

Sometimes by night the children seem innocuous.
Sometimes I forget they broke my tailbone
and it never healed right. They sleep in curled up heaps
blankets pooled on the floor. I reapply the blankets.
Tirelessly patrol. They are sabotaging me, I'm sure of it.

Their faces look like when they were babies. Tomorrow
their brows will furrow and someone will be
called an asshole and probably hit with a ball. Tonight
they pretend to be secret angels, testing mortals on earth.

The women at the park direct their children's play.
Their kids go to them to settle fights and give them money,
my kids know not to ask me, climbing the equipment,
they yell their independence across the sand, by saying nothing

and the women wrinkle their eyes at me
as if to ask, "Where is your helicopter?" And I wonder
if their days don't often play over and over and over
in a loop like a CD I used to like in junior high?

Last summer, I sat in the swings at one a.m., waiting for
the night to wear out of me, waiting for sleep
to feel like a friend. In the dark blue, a couple appeared
by the biggest tree. Leaning against it

kissing against it, he put her head in his hands, as if to crush it
but kissed her instead, crushed her lips against his
her body disappearing behind his
until they heard the chain of my swing cling
and walked off quickly. When I draw the park now
as I watch the sunshine kids play, I think of this couple
her head in his hands, her body
crushed against the dark tree
almost invisible now.

Marcy's Diner

They say online she ordered three full pancakes
for her toddler. They say it was too much
for a baby, it took too long, the baby was crying.

They say the owner slammed her hands on the table
and screamed in the baby's face, You need to shut the hell up!
like a cop drama, breaking the suspect.

Almost two years old, the child should have known
that this was not the space to want pancakes too much
or be frustrated still when they finally come.

Almost two years old, she should have known
how to sit straight and still. She should have known
time and had her briefcase handy.

They say parents should stay home if they have kids
who cry. Lock themselves in the recesses of their
living rooms or always remove their children outside.

I remember my daughter wailing in a restaurant
in Chinatown. Nothing I could give her would console her:
toys, snacks, keys, a pen and a receipt.

She was two and she wasn't going to be held or put down.
She wasn't going to sit or go outside. She didn't like
the bathroom or running up and down the empty steps.

She was two and life had been bad to her and nobody
could understand so she screamed her sorrow
to every stranger who passed on the sidewalk

struggling to get out of my arms, my food becoming

a tv dinner, my day becoming a prison
of bedroom walls. My life becoming

three full pancakes. And I wonder if that mother grazes
on her child's chicken nuggets the way I do mine, if she wanted
the pancakes in a box To Go for the car – a more quiet ride

home where she should stay, they say,
she shouldn't have ordered so many,
they say, she should take the baby outside
until the kid is old enough to pay
taxes and have a job and learn what it is like
to eat three full pancakes

in a public space.

SCARED OF THE DARK

It's the time of night
when even dogs sleep quietly
and the crickets are louder
than the cars. The TV is on mute
and the fan spins unstably overhead.
I have read every email, liked every
Facebook post, nobody wants
to chat. It's the time of night
I start to feel very uneasy
about being me, about what I said
the day before last Thursday
and I think if only I could stop myself
from ever speaking, everything would be
alright. It's the time of night
every floor in my house creaks in pain
and if it didn't complain today, it would
tomorrow because we're all getting older,
it says. And I want to argue remodel, but
it reminds me of my credit. It's the time of night
I realize my house is right and resign
myself to crow's feet. It's the time of night
my bills puff themselves up in their piles so
they are taller than the tomatoes. I want to band
them in a stack or burn them but I can't stand
the sight of them. It's the time of night
I picture my children running off a cliff –
falling from a mountain top
or being sucked into a tornado,
dropping from a Ferris wheel, kidnapped
by strangers, hit by a car, then drowned. It's the time of night
I sneak into their rooms and sometimes
I take pictures because nine only lasts for one year
and days have passed already. I put blankets over their toes

because of frostbite. It's the time of night
when darkness is heavy and I get worried so I reach out
to turn on the light, thinking maybe
if the corners weren't so dark, honey and tea
would be enough to calm me and I could sleep
without wondering what else is breaking.

How to Be the Final Girl

Never fall in love
finally. The music will end and
everyone will go home.
Your relationship will become
irrelevant. You will become
irrelevant, until you birth babies who have
their own stories and you play a supporting
role instead, some woman who endlessly offers
tea and refills muffin trays. If you are a woman
you will shrivel into a stereotype
and roll through the credits
pretty and poised, in tenth place, nine places behind
your husband.

Don't wear glasses.
You look better without them. Put on makeup
to be noticed. It helps to be a cheerleader
with a ponytail or a nerd who takes her ponytail down
at the end of the school year. It helps to be impressed
by high school boys, cars, romantic clichés.

Wear heels when you run,
they accentuate
your resolve to escape.

Never walk alone
at night under lamplights
unless you are a cat or man.
Don't jingle your keys like some invitation
to find you. Don't think of what lurks
behind bushes and closed doors.
Never call a cab
the driver might have a hidden

knife. Never have your own car
someone is under the back seat. Never call a girlfriend –
there is nothing two women can do
better than one. Never call a boyfriend –
he might be the one following you.

Never make tea. You will die.
Watch, put a kettle on and wait for it
to whistle. There will be a gun or knife.
Someone you love will
attack you. I'm sorry to tell you
you shouldn't have put the carrot-knife down or opened
your heart. I am sorry to tell you
you shouldn't close the bathroom mirror.
Everything private or relaxing should be
avoided. Especially if you're a woman living
alone.

What We Do In Binghamton

We let our dogs roam the backyards guarding against
squirrels. They are brave in the face of cats, but wind
is a brute and leaves are psychotic killers. We build
snowwomen. Sad ones. We rank number one in
pessimism and complain about it. It is impossible to find
a psychiatrist. There are no open spaces. No parking
at the University. No space on Parade Day. No parking
during the art walk, on First Friday. There's
a painting called "Grandmother," with a wrinkled smile propping
up green eyes. Next to it, an unnamed display of a ferret
pelt on top scattered light bulbs. We have traffic half –
circles, but all our other portions are large. We don't want
your hydrofrack. Sometimes we just have to
put on a moustache. Sometimes it's a snow day and we
use up all the saved stickers on one poster. It can be lonely
during the winter so you better have a big
family. We have pools in the summer when the snow finally
shrivels in black heaps and disappears. Only 50 cents. And our trees
are green; they know good customer service now. We wait for our
mail and watch a tree dance for us. Make mental notes for
improvements. Stand in line behind 30 others for regular soft serve.
We watch it all die too. Call that death beautiful
before we curse the cycle because we're cold, not because we're
altruistic. We say goodbye to baby toys. Dora has found a *nuevo amiga y*
everyone moves on. We learn about the Iroquois. There will be
a long house or a rattle or something else made from
paper mache and glitter, just as the Iroquois did it, and at the end
of the year parents will date their children to a dance. We will
wait for them to date for real and pretend the texting
means zero. Our kids cross the train tracks to get to the Red &
White for junk food. We find a sole shoe abandoned outside
Price Chopper. This is where the goldfish cracker was last month.
Change is inevitable. The kids walk to the Red & White

and when they come back they sit on the porch and talk about going away to college. They want to stay here, except the ones who want to leave more than breathe. Even they will be back.

TWO PIECES OF BREAD

He picks up the kids
from his mother's house
after waiting on customers
for eight hours
and going to school
for two.
I take them to the daycare
every other week
when we have the money.
He fixes all the broken
parts of our life
with duct tape
and used parts.
I sell the old clothes
the kids outgrow
for new-to-you used ones
and butter and milk.
Our children spill from the seams
of our house, bite up the furniture
tear down our walls
and identities.
We keep pushing together,
no way to unstick now.

CICADAS

Brood II is coming. The 17-year Cicadas.
Last time they visited was the summer
we got married. And like something
in Aesop's fables we spent
all our laundry money on stuffed crust
pizzas and I had to wash
my tights in the sink come winter.
I don't remember if you washed
anything, but I think that's the point.

In year one there were the white cats,
placed on my chest while I was sleeping.
Beyond a princess dream to wake up
to kittens crawling all over me. But also
my thrown purse and the toaster oven apology,
ten-years in use (R. I. P.) to balance
the checkbook we didn't keep.

Year two we bought our first house. Put up a Christmas
tree. For a gift I got a bunch of glass
shelves to put things on, so people could look
at them. By year 3 I'd had a birthday party
and got some things to fill a shelf, but people
were always asking me about a

baby now. When are you going to have a
baby? They asked it like it was milk
chocolate. Go get it at the grocery! Why didn't I
have this already? Why was I against getting it? Just
do it! But my body failed me. I was waiting
to burst from the dirt and do my biological duty.
My primary doctor gave me a referral.

The cicadas stay underground all those years
just to surface and mate and die. For cicadas, youth
is long, but once an adult it's molt,
lay eggs and croak. The middle-aged
cicada sees her future and she screams
but the sound is drowned by the mating call
and after awhile everyone is tired of the drama
and they get to work. After I didn't get pregnant

we went to a specialist. He hung oranges
from my ovaries as ovulation drugs. I cried for
hit-and-run animals and my uterus ached like it got caught
in the car door. After a year and nine months
we had our first girl. I got more
things to put on the shelves

and through years 5,6,7,8, 9 we got another
girl and a boy. We got a car payment. We got a swing
set. We threw away
our diaper genie and every wall in our home
was crayoned. The rocking chair had teeth
marks all over the arms. All payments started coming out
of our account automatically. Actually living life costs
an extra fifty bucks a month.
We can't afford it. By year

heart disease, it's hard to remember
when I last saw you or my phone number. Heart failure
can do that to memory, the doctor tells me
in the hospital. You ask if we can have sex
and I hope you don't mean at the hospital.
I'm wishing I could have a glass of red
but I'm not to drink anymore. My mother brings
you alcohol to the hospital as a birthday present.
Scotch of course. Johnny Walker Black. I still remember

wondering if anyone would notice if I'd snagged
a Dixie cup. Now I don't need it. I'm on

the right medications. I have a few coping
plans. I'm trying to teach them to our children:
Ten deep breaths before the state test. I know
the cicadas are coming to sing, but I don't know their
language and if it matches ours? I don't know if you remember
the old songs we sang? Or if gum in my arm hair would seem
funny anymore? I don't know if I can flap my wings
like I used to, or if after molting too many times I'm tired
of the whole ballroom dance? Spring means

revival from the ground and I feel like singing
loudly with the cicada men and lying heavy on
wet leaves. I feel like standing in the rain
firmly and sprouting toward the sun like a blade
of grass that's curved to love herself in a hug. And
maybe if I do these things I will feel new again
like a Phoenix who's so old she's young.

How To Get An "A"

Four months of cough syrup
and my chest was still swimming.
A new bottle costs a co-pay
and I pay it thinking
this will be the thing
that makes me better.

I have stopped using the measuring cup.
I can tell the tablespoons
by feel. One tongue and a half is the dose
and it coats my throat as I sink
into my bed to watch the ceiling spin.
I have done this day again and again.

In the morning I will go to class
hacking in the hallways
and napping my lunch.
I can't eat.
Figure I'm just out of shape.
I don't notice that I've lost weight.
I go home and read myself
to codeine sleep. There is no time
for food or fun. There is school
and there is cough syrup. Soon I must

stop between classes. I am out of breath
and can't walk down the hall without sitting.
I can't walk up or down stairs.
I'm embarrassed to be. I don't know my phone
number. I drove over a curb. I almost
hit the Stop sign. I sat at the daycare staring
at a clock for 4 hours in a rocking chair.

The day the doctor told me my heart was failing
my husband drove me to the hospital.
In the waiting room I sprawled my body
across the chair and table sinking to the floor
before they scooped me to my room.

When I was stable, with flowers lining the windows
talking about a pacemaker instead of a transplant
I asked if I could have
my schoolbooks.

HE SAID SOMETHING ABOUT HEMINGWAY

He said something about Hemingway
while I'm frozen on the metal table
with my head turned to the right
always to the right and they are drilling on the left
or it feels like drilling and it makes a noise
like a screw spinning in wood and it tugs like a dentist
after a numb tooth. It is pull, tug, pull on my
collarbone. I imagine someone slams the door
with a string tied to my chest making
the bones come loose and spin on the floor.

I tried to ask, "What about Hemingway?"
but the drugs had changed the shape of my mouth
and the right sounds wouldn't come out.
The doctor patted my head and said, "It's Ok."
But I wanted to know what he was saying about
Hemingway and I wanted to tell them I didn't
like the tugging. Or the swarm of nurses
in white scrubs swishing coldness past
me as they checked my IV stuck in a naked
body under a thin sheet of blue paper.

I felt a sharp stab. I heard myself whimper.
Then a rush of calm again. Cold again. I had been
re-drugged and Hemingway was concise. Like surgery.
And there was always dialogue and very little setting
like these white people in this white room.
A clean well-lighted place and electroshock therapy
to help the depression and the lonely bed
and my cold metal table stung me and I wondered if he
liked the cold metal of the guns he played with
until he finally used one to end the tug.

Maybe this is what they were saying. Maybe one day I would use a typewriter and a shot glass and everyone would say I was like Hemingway and even the nurses who scoffed at the idea in surgery will tell the doctor, "Yes yes, she was like Hemingway after all."

And just before the drugs wear off I feel a sudden shock to my chest. A test. To see if the treatment was working.

Doctor's Orders

The mask was supposed to help me breathe.
It went up my nose, around my face
like fat fingers that made me feel
I couldn't scream. I kept taking
it off while the nurses worried I must wear it all the time.
Mask strapped to my face
I had ambein dreams of a lake to lie in
where the still water
closed around my throat
until I felt I was Ophelia
floating so much like a ribbon
that death seemed the most beautiful
plot device. But as the water crept down my throat
it tasted bitter and I startled awake.

I threw the mask to my side table
stacked with sixteen hand-made cards
from my daughter's second-grade class.
Each child hoping in her own words
I'd be well soon. I imagined the instructions
chalked on the board. A prescription:
What to include and in which form.
I was the life lesson her class was given.
Sick is sad. But so are fragments.
I thought of my daughter collecting
sixteen supportive cards to bring to the hospital
and wondered if they made her backpack heavy
if they strained her shoulders. I wondered
if she felt their weight pulling her under
like the grip of the ocean, no longer able
to float.

Becoming Binghamtonian

A tree stretches her branches like she's trying
an idea for the first time. The wind shakes
everything like the train is passing again.
Snow falls in bonded patches.

I found a scarf at the thrift, long enough to be
a boa constrictor. I wrapped it around my neck
like I wanted to stop breathing. I let it spin
and fall and trip and bleed.

Outside, each speck of snow is really just
an army. Each time the phone rings, it is really just
an assault. My mother leaves me a message
to stop ignoring her. I click my phone ignore.

I put my books in a broken washer who lives
on my porch. I needed the books close by while I
wrote my thesis. Even the Sun slept
in that broken washer for the summer.

I'd flip through articles about the birth of a spiedie
and how the alliance of rivers was formed, they say
"confluence," and it sounds like something to have
a martini over, so I have five.

Carousels make me feel I am moving, I'm free
until they lurch to a halt and my stomach stops
spinning and I'm just another person staggering
through the park, no direction.

In 1975, three firemen drowned trying to save
people at Rockbottom Dam. The Susquehanna
River rolls people under the water and then

lets them back up for one last breath.

The instinct is to swim up, fight the dam, but the device
keeps beating you down. The only way out is under;
to swim to the bottom, let the water take you,
push you through.

This is how you become from Binghamton.

SATURDAY IN PAJAMAS

Saturday nights always dim slower than the week and fill
with the smell of berries and tea and incense pulled
through open windows. Saturday fans spin air everywhere
like balloons untied in the bedroom. My hair twirls to the side
of my eyes and I think I look pretty again. If I only stare
at my hair I can look pretty again. Before I got married,

when I was young. Before the kids came. Before the anti
depressants and the anxiety medications. Before the heart
failure. Before I went on a date when I was sixteen, I spent
an hour on my hair. I put on make-up. I used to go to the mall
to get the right earrings. But it became tiring to do the things
I did before I knew who I was. Saturdays can sigh at sunset

now. I will probably watch the moon rise out my window
from my side of the bed. I don't want to admit how much time
I spend sitting here in this safe place. Sometimes when it's sad out,
I can sleep myself to Sunday from this exact spot. I used to lie
in my closet when I got upset, wrap blankets around my shoulders, lock
myself in. But doors aren't needed if the blankets are wrapped
tight enough. Bed frames become boundaries too.

For Keith
(and William Carlos Williams)

This is just to say
I dropped half a pop
tart in the bottom of the
toaster around 2am, first in
small chunks
then in bigger patches and
finally a thin,
long
chocolate
beam speeding past the
metal jaws meant
to prey on bread or processed
food. I was going to fish the long

tart pieces out with a knife but
then I thought I remembered
that this was a bad idea and I should
Google it. I also
didn't mean to
drop my necklace down
the drain yesterday.
Everything I touch
has become
depressed.
I'll let you know
what the Google results for
"knife" and "toaster"
return.

How to Talk to Me in Bed

I'm sorry that I hate
the shape of my face
and the slide of my nose.
I'm sorry that I flinch when you say,
You're beautiful or lick
my ankles.
I'm sorry that I hide
under blankets,
that I make you chase me
to the edges of the bed,
and then I play dead
or disinterested. I'm sorry
I don't know my name
and I hate everything you can call me.
I'm sorry I can't stand my stomach
and how our children
have destroyed it,
that I can't see its curve
as you do,
and that the way you see it
is worse to me
than the way I do.
I'm sorry I want to cry
instead. I want to cry
instead.

If you would just pull my hair,
harder. I think
it could work. If you could just
pretend to care
a little less,
this could kill me nicely. If you could

find it in your heart
to hate me enough,
things would be nearly
perfect.

How To Be Manic

Talk loudly about how much you love to dance
or even louder about how you hate your mother
in law. When your friends ask you to lower your
voice, tell them to 'fuck off.' Sing every song as if

you were the artist. Believe it's something you
could really do, after all you did 6th grade choir and
a musical in high school. Decide to become
a singer and actress. Decide to dress in your high

school clothes. The skirt won't zip up so untuck
the shirt. Lie in bed and wait for your husband
or your boyfriend or your girlfriend or have an
affair. Have sex and then have sex and then have

a speed down the highway because you will never
die. After all, you haven't yet and so you can't. Decide
maybe you're not human. Maybe you are something
else. Maybe you can sprout cat ears and a tail for balance.

Maybe you can limp along fence posts and blend
with the night. Maybe you can become invisible
before jumping into the sun and lying in a beam.
Feel a rumble in your belly that won't go away.

It rumbles in your head. Throw a rusted training
wheel down your driveway, drink too much Scotch
to slow your thoughts. Remember how much you hate
yourself. Think it might be sensible to cut yourself

and let the anger leak out. Practice on your pinky
to see how deep you can make yourself go. Make it
a contest. Make it up to yourself with vodka when you
get tired of creating new finger prints.

WHAT THE CHEMICALS WANT

I will stay awake forever, sleep stealing time
no need to shower
this week, I can drink so much I don't recall
how I got home
I can sleep for months if it becomes
necessary to understand why I need
and need and need and need more
I will take more and ask for more and give
nothing, but doll eyes
I will pretend I don't have bills, doctor's
appointments, children
I will tell people to *fuck off* openly
elitist, mean, insincere people
or friends
I will make special signs for the university
and hang them in the Lecture Hall
wait for a fight
or go to an Internet message board
argue about the price of a highchair
I will hear my name
everywhere I go and feel people saying
nice or mean things
I will drink compliments like coffee
I will feel compliments burn my cheeks hide my face with hair
I will cover the mirrors in my room with towels
hate every part of myself like a chanted prayer
I will never be everything/ anything
this hurts me daily
I will not pay my speeding tickets
get another warrant
I will play a song on repeat for a week
it will become the only true thing
about me, this movie playing

83.

and I am the lead
or the director who controls the moon and sun
I will stitch myself into my sheets, no light
I will make my life explode
like something hot and bright and beautiful

Wanted: People or Person

Wanted: Someone to hang out with me when I'm mad about memes. Wanted: Someone who knows the difference between Veronica Mars and Sherlock Holmes. Wanted: Kristen Bell. Wanted: Someone who knows the music, since I have the lyrics covered. Wanted: Someone to drive me to the bank and the doctor and the university. Payment in ginger tea or french kisses, your choice. Wanted: Hate notes in calligraphy. Wanted: Stay in your own lane or crash into mine like a wave that wears me down into something level and even. Wanted: Someone to stay in the car when I run toward the red light screaming; someone to stay seated when I dance on the table; someone to stay in the waiting room when I go to Planned Parenthood; someone to stay. Wanted: Someone who doesn't want to break everything breakable. Wanted: Someone who doesn't need to mend everything that's broken. Wanted: Read Jane Eyre and tell me we are like that twisted tree. Wanted: Someone who reads books I don't know, but doesn't make me feel dumb about it. Wanted: Someone who listens to what I read, but doesn't make me feel dumb about it. Wanted: No republicans. Wanted: My curls bunch like they are natural; my boobs are smooshed together like they are fake; I make up the truth like I can write. Wanted: For the mirror to answer back, "You're the ugliest of them all." Wanted: When I was in 5th grade, I had a long skirt with vertical, rainbow stripes around it. I knew if I could spin like a top, a rainbow would swallow me up. It was hand-me-down and meant for a woman of 40 in 1960. I wore it constantly, spinning spinning, always spinning a rainbow around me when I wore it. One day I heard a group of girls snickering about how out of date my skirt was, how stupid it looked. Wanted: Spinning before I heard those girls talking.

How to Fall in Love With a Straight Woman

Close your eyes. You don't have to try to think of her, she just appears, across the table in Composition Theory on Tuesdays and Thursdays. Try to get into her group. Sit at the outskirts quietly while a curtain of brown hair lets in the sun and then covers her face. Try not to make her mad, she gets mad and gorgeous easily.

Stalk her on MySpace. She loves Texas. You don't. You can work through this. She loves Jesus. You really don't. You can work through this. She likes "Men." You are not men.

When she finds out you are the "H is for Hiding from Nuns" from the Internet blog, feel your face heat to boil as she talks of you to others in the group. "She's so funny!" slamming her hand on the table. Smile and look down, because touching eyes is painful. Smile and look down because funny only comes from finger tips. Take the paper she gives you at the end of the class, folded up scrap, creased and smeared with ink, a phone number, a date, "a party," she drops it in your hand.

Feel sick and full of lightning bugs. Feel ill and lit up from within. Close your eyes, close your eyes or the light will seep out in the hallway.

Learn to drink with your husband at a free hotel happy hour years before. Drink red wine and red wine until your toes feel like the tips of fire that spirals up the chimney, escaping to live somewhere wild.

Get to the party and take a large glass of red. Sit next to her on the back porch swing. See patio chairs of people around you, playing "I've Never" and other high school games you've never played. Too serious. No interest in unsanctioned risk or stupidity.

But today you play. You've never been to Canada. You've never had that drink, "Sex on the Beach." You've never bargained for a better grade. You've never asked for an extension. You've never written the paper the day it was due. You've never asked anyone for the answers. You've only cheated for elementary school love. They make you drink anyway. You've never been arrested. You've never been suspended. You've never been on academic probation. You've never had a cavity and people are getting annoyed now. You've never dated an English major, you've never dated a professor, you've never kissed a woman.

Watch her drink her beer, like she kissed her whole high school. Hold your untouched wine as she pushes heavy hair from her face, pulls you in like a secret, and kisses you.

Feel the Gertrude Stein fly fly your finger tips fly fly from your finger tips fly from wherever inside you that you don't know you have. Feel her tongue tell your body what to do. Feel her hair through your fingers and try not to pull. Feel your seating arrangement change. Feel around for your bearings when she starts to pull away. Send an atheist's prayer that she does it again.

Drink when she tells you to.

Become the girl everyone dares her to kiss. Become the girl to dare to kiss. Come up with elaborate scenarios as to why you should make out. Sometimes she will say okay. Clip your hair clip to her swing and forget about it until forever. Kiss her when people are watching because she's less likely to kiss you when you're alone. You can work through this.

Kiss her at parties, spinning dizzy like a tornado. Kiss her on the swing, pulling back and flying high in the tornado. Kiss her in the kitchen, against the cabinets, in the hallway, against the wall, on the couch, lying on a corner as she strips for you when everyone else has gone home. Only touch where she puts your hands.

She sits on your lap, she takes off her shirt. She turns the music up. Only touch where she puts your hands. She doesn't like girls, want to go that far, it's just for fun and play, she says.

Listen to her say she doesn't want to do it so much. Watch her pull away, fall for a tall guy with traditional tastes. Watch them love Texas together. Watch him be nice and respectable. Hate him.

Try to make out with her until the guy she's dating says he doesn't like it. Try to kiss her anyway. Try not to cry. Try to make her mad. Have too much to drink. Lick her shoulder. Try to remember to pick up your clip but forget. Have another drink and slosh it around, like a hurricane. Cry. Try to make her eyes flash at you - mad or anything.

Try to close your eyes. She will disappear. She will be a friend or network connection in the near future. She will have half traditional kids who love Jesus and Texas. The swing will rust and the clip will be stolen by a squirrel. She will barely remember making out with you, laughing like the secret was real, how that part ended. She will be a good professional contact. She will be a good reflective reminder. She will be filed under, *Firestarter.*

So You Will Know Me

I discard my laundry down the hall
like Gretel's trail of breadcrumbs
so I can find my way back
to the bedroom. I leave cherry
stems in ashtrays, tied up in kinky
knots. I leave bottles of perfume, or
Scrubbing Bubbles, or Raid by the bed
to fend off any would-be-murderers
who will try to kill me in my sleep. I am
cautious. I've seen hundreds of scary
movies. I already know the boyfriend
did it. I'm not scared of the dark, just
the knife flying through it. Sometimes
I take my dogs downstairs just to get
water at night. Sometimes I wake my
husband up because I hear tornados. We
live in upstate New York. Sometimes I
can't watch the news and so I watch
YouTube videos of kittens. I can watch
kittens fumble to walk for half a day.
I can train a cat to sit and high five me.
I can tell their mood based on their
tail's twitch. I know about cicadas and
dogs and bees too. G.I. Joe says
knowing is half the battle. We can talk about
how the mouth forms a vowel. We can
talk about local politics or writing or
poverty or farms. We can pretend not to
hear our phones together. We can let them
drain of battery life and lose them. We
can strum a G chord (it's the only one
I know). We can dance in the parking lot
when the bar closes. Nobody's here

to drown the moon. I will dance like a rag
doll, and you will find me floppy. I will
make a face like a fish but I think
it's like a lizard, but you say fish and I want you
to be happy so I say it's a fish too. I want you
to be happy with me, so I dance for you
and say fish and tilt my head to seem
pretty. I tilt my head and wait for you
to know me.

-for Lisa

Rapid Cycling

the sky shouts her blue
hosts white clouds, puff-painted
and twirled with joy
my fence, linked
to old ideas and gates never
opened, asks to die
Joni Mitchell is too slow
and Britney Spears and Linkin Park -
only Liszt can hope
to catch me
the wind
is swirling my words
in a dance
everything is like the first
bite, the first drag, the first
word, first drink, first
god

What Kind of Person Are You: Take the Quiz!

You Got: Marzipan person with a metal knife hidden inside. You got: Most likely to be stood up, sitting at the bar at Zippers. You got: Diseased. You got: No shoulder pads. You got: Still awake at 6 a.m., writing poems for the trash, clothes all over your floor and a piece of pizza on your night stand. No plate. You got: Left alone all weekend as a child, green bean dinner, powdered milk, the apartment has Skinimax, "Weekend at Bernie's" plays so often you memorize it, you don't know the names of the other movies, you don't listen to the words. You got: Watch "Embrace of the Vampire" so often you fall in love with Alyssa Milano. And vampires. You got: Jane Eyre means everything. You got: Folders, binders, pens, pencils, markers, flash drives, crayons, notebooks. You got: Buy everything. You got: Alice in Wonderland, DRINK ME. You got: Sick: one day hitting a curb and a stop sign in slow motion, 2 miles an hour, tied to a hospital bed by oxygen tubes up your nose, heart trying to die, no salt, no salt, watch your water intake too, no alcohol anymore, walk because running will bleed everything through. You got: Drunk and running in the street, bleeding energy from every surface, red wine spilling all over your white dress.

I Always Drive Over Potholes

leave the mayonnaise out
overnight, blue lid flung
carelessly on a table of toast crumbs
I drip mustard on the white shirt
you washed just last night
and hung up in your quarter of the closet
I drop cookies
in the bottom of the oven
let my cheese bubble over
the blue bowl, onto
the base of the microwave
I leave the water running
as I walk out of the room
talking on the phone
about the benefits of technology
I turn your socks pink
by throwing read panties in the wash
I get loud when I'm drunk
I get drunk when I'm bored
I sing along to every song
that plays on the radio
and when you join in
I correct you on the lyrics
I take your boxers
and wear them as pajamas
I lecture about equality, while cooing
I do not know how to work the VCR, dishwasher,
lawnmower, water heater, I do not know
how to push spiders away or our garbage day
I put your Sinatra CD in my
Alanis case, and when I'm done
with Alanis I leave
Sinatra teetering on top the TV

I spill my pizza
tip my soda
and break the bottle of Hennessey
on the back porch, but
you do not yell
only sweep shards of glass
across wet pavement and say
Don't cry over spilt Brandy.

CHICKEN TACOS

Two days til pay day and we scrape together a dollar and twelve cents. The bananas have fallen off the plastic tree and there is only one apple left. The garlic stands alone.

The weather has been temperamental and so I grab a sweatshirt. By the time we get to the truck it's snowing. The snow sticks to my clothes like static and looks like mothballs. I swat it off me because I want the Spring to come so badly.

In the grocery, we look at the row of peppers. $3.99 a pound. The jalapeño is obvious. Nothing can be done without it. My husband picks a fat one and weighs it. It rolls around on the scale and I want to crunch into it with milk.

Now there is a choice. With thirty cents gone, we must be cautious. He eyes a serrano. It's small. It looks hot. "This is the one," he holds it out to the grocery lights and we look at it for a moment, silently.

As we scan each pepper in the self-check out, we laugh at our good fortune. Two days until pay day and we still have a chicken breast and lettuce and corn tortillas. Two days until pay day and we found a dollar and twelve cents just to spend on peppers alone.

We insert sixty-four cents and grab our receipt. For some reason, the amount amuses us. We continue to laugh as we pass the bagging attendant, the shopping cart collector, the people in the parking lot pushing off the mothball snow. We keep laughing as we run to the truck, pretending we stole the serrano, that we would be caught by the jalapeño council. Held in a cold cell for food processing. So we decide we will run from Winter until Spring comes. And when Winter is done snowing, we will make fire.

HEATHER WANTS TO INVEST $40 000

It says so on Google. I type in Heather wants
and it tells me this is it. It must be the reason my dreams always end
with his funeral (the one I didn't attend) and why I pull the covers
over my ears so I can't hear the memory of him saying, "If I were her,
I'd be just like her," as he tosses a pillow past me to his office couch.
As he steals the air from his office fan for his own beard. As he jokes
about Britney Spears and modesty, as he throws around
the rubber chicken. As he says he is "the midwife to my ideas,
but [I] have to get [myself] pregnant."

Heather wants a great orgasm story – or any great
story, Heather wants to grab his booty!, Heather
wants to solve poverty through better design, Heather wants
a fairy tale ending. This is why I can't read
that email with the final poem he wrote before he died.
This is why the poem is stiff in my Inbox like the carcass of a crow.
It's called "Open Heart," written just before his closed.
I can't read it until I am done with my PhD. Maybe until I have tenure.
I can't read it because it probably doesn't remember me.

Heather wants your man. Heather wants cake.
Heather wants you to succeed and she wants to help!
Heather lies in bed and reads crumpled papers
filled with old poems, each signed to her with a note. She traces
the words with wide eyes, seeing symbols in the torn corners
and smudged ink. There are clues in the way an "L" is shaped.

When Heather closes the bathroom mirror, she expects him to pop
up behind her and yell, "Funny joke, huh?!" Heather wants answers
about almond butter.

THANKS TO THE GIDEONS

One night, crying and smoking in the hotel bathroom
with the shower running steam onto the mirror
the fan whirring insomnia
I got an idea for a poem about death and rain.

I had no paper, so I took the Bible
from the top drawer of the side table
and wrote over the first three sheets
with a hotel pen until a thin page tore

then I wrote some more and put it back
for someone else to find. I was giddy with the thought
of someone mad or intrigued or even laughing
at how bad my lines were.

Since then, I have used most hotel Bibles
for self-publishing. Sometimes I mark out words
leaving only the ones I like, to create found poems.
Sometimes I go to the verses I hate –

stonings, slavery, [almost] killing your kid,
and mark them in red, note them in the front:
"turn to [page x or page y]," sometimes I wrap
the Bible in a poem, like the first time

with smoke and thunder and drooping eyes that can't
stop thinking. Or sometimes I just read the book of Ruth.
Imagine what it means for sisterhood, and put the Bible back
in the top drawer tired, remembering that women

have always been resourceful.

THE HAPPY GENIUS OF MY HOUSEHOLD

People don't approve of my affair
with the moon. You must have to get up
with the children, they say, You must
be home to cook breakfast and dinner.

Some nights I don't need sleep. I read
from my bibliographies
take the dog for a walk, if I'm brave,
mostly write. It's the only time
nobody needs me. It's the only time it feels
safe to work and nobody

is calling me. And I can listen to Icona Pop
"I Love It" 21 times and nobody
is stopping me. There is nobody
on the trampoline, there is nobody
on the back porch with a loud friend,
nobody is untucked. The sun is coming up

and this makes me sad. If I were an octopus
I might never need to rest. I could squeeze out of my tank,
unarmed and solitary. I once heard about
an octopus who stole fish by night.
By day she drove her kids to swim
and picked them up from gymnastics.

My mother shamed me for not
watching my kids' sports practices.
My Inbox will bling all day until 11 pm.
The alarms for my meetings squawk like birds.
But by midnight the air is death.
How can I sleep in such sweet absence?

20 Goals

I want to know how to tie knots. They might keep me in place. I want to know how to win friends and influence people. To remember dates and forget conversations that play overandoverandover in my head. To pretend I believe in anything, even god or crystals powered by the moon; horoscopes or ghosts who need me to help them to the other side. To wear the red heels, the strappy heels, the clear heels that light when I click-step to the mailbox in the black dress that matches. I want to sleep in them, wake up late and fall out of bed to meetings, lighting the halls. I want to take your girlfriend, I like her breath. To take your boyfriend, I like his hands. To keep my husband, I love his everything. To forget my mistakes. They are like trick candles. To repeat my mistakes. They are like too much cake. Too much cake. Too much cake. I want to be made from a page. Perfectly lined letters. I want to finish what I've finished. I want to remember what I've hidden and be known for my talent for destruction.

How to Read

I like to pretend I have a soul and that my soul
drinks with Charles Darwin's soul on a train ride
while outside the rain pounds the grass down
and makes the world soggy and rainbow bright
ready for a new mutation.

My soul would sneak into the library after closing
and make a bed of paperbacks, piled like fall leaves
she would slip between the pages while she dreamed.
Maybe she would walk through the mud with Elizabeth
Bennett. Maybe she would go drinking in London with
Karim Amir. She might go to Lowood with Jane, go to the city
with Esther, or to meet Gwendolyn Brooks at the microfiche
machine to argue alliteration or slant rhyme.

If I had a soul, she would be the troubled kind. She would
go to court-ordered therapy and have angry outbursts
over empty ice cream pints and stolen knitted shawls.
She would try to convince you of the patterns
in the wall, clawing to stay in. If I had a soul she would be
the damned kind. I'm no good at religion and it feels too good
to burn myself.

So much depends

upon the table
pills

rattle roll spill
swallow

sleep to dream
voices

stars are just
stars.

I WOULD RATHER NOT SLEEP

It's too hot and my head isn't ready
for medication and bed. I am
a brilliance. I want to be
for ever/yone and I will be so swirly
you will think of me like leaves
in Fall that left home
but tried to come back. I just
want to hold on for a little bit.
That was two hours ago, but I have to
stay awake. I have to snap my body
like a branch so I won't bend.
Sleep will drag my eyes shut again
but it's been two days. I can fight
for awhile more but I am
dangerously close to cycling
down the stairs
to where the people talk in my head
about how they don't like me.

Twenty Year Vows

I.
I gave you Chinese food, vegetables, enchiladas.
I gave you a place to be: watching me practice

my high school play, making out
in a dark car, wherever you could be

but church or college. Now I give you a brand new
Tuesday, never redone. I give you a ride to Sonic

when you're drunk. I give you a place to complain
about work and space to keep working. I smash your

habits when they spin like the washer. I give you wild
books and plot twists. I break your routine

splintered like glass. I break your life so it can never
look the same again, so I'm fused to your bones.

II.
You give me eggs and bacon every day. You give me
chili gravy, chocolate covered Oreos and Southern Comfort

peanuts on Mother's Day. You give me an alarm
a daily wake-up, a one-more-warning.

You give me a place to be nothing and left alone
like something exceptional.

You give me a place to be worthless and covered
in blankets and pillows. You give me

a pocket to be kept in or let go. You give me a buoy
to return to, an ocean to sink through,

a lifejacket that looks like
a weight.

INVISIBILITY STUDIES

I tell them about my pacemaker
as we walk up jagged rocks
because I'm the same age as they are
and their eyes seem to question why
I can't step up steep hills without
losing my breath.
I want them to slow a bit
and let me catch up, just to listen
when I say I better turn back early
because I'm already tired
instead of insisting
we all wait and go together.

We walk hard up hills and I become
a cherry tomato. People finally start
to slow and I slip on mossy rocks
my leg tumbles into the stream
between two boulders. Someone else
is impatient. He needs to be at work
while my leg is bleeding
and I'm having trouble breathing. Earlier

that day, we sat down for a barbeque
and to skip stones in the stream below.
It was a steep walk down the rocks
and I walked barefoot, the stream
stabbing my feet with its pointed pebbles.

At the base we gathered in the pool of water
and selected the smoothest stones, the ones
most likely to propel themselves,
to fly straight, to get into the best colleges. I sat
in the shallow shore water, picking up rocks

105.

washed perfect by force.
We all threw the rough rocks we found
like balled up paper, a mistake, into the center
of the pond.

Sitting in the pool of water judging rocks
we bond over the odd shapes of the sharp
stones before discarding them. One looks
like Idaho before it's thrown away
into the center. Everyone sees that it was Idaho
and the round rocks have no names.

Later, when someone is late for work and
I'm out of breath and bleeding,
I see bees floating through tall grass
like kites pushed frantic by rough wind.
The others are watching the time

instead. The next week, on campus
I park in a handicapped spot
and hang my permit on my mirror.
A woman drives up and asks me:
Are you even disabled? I tell her I am
and point to my hanging tag
swinging on my mirror. She speeds away
yelling: *Well you don't look it!*

SELFIE #9

I look in the mirror and become
a Klingon. I have a beautiful ridged
forehead and a sexy growl. I look
in the mirror and become a vamp-
ire. I have bloody fangs that taste
like sex and success. I look in the past
and I have shaky legs, high heels, a god
and a step-father. I look in my back
seat and see blankets, bottles,
lollipop sticks, pressed to the dirty
carpet. I look in my front
pocket and find tangled string that threads
through my ears and carries
ugly words, threading ugly sounds, threading
words through my head. I look in the future
and I can't see that far.

HEATHER DORN WAS BORN WITH A PLASTIC SPORK IN HER MOUTH. AS A CHILD HER MOTHER WOULD TAKE HER TO TACO BELL AND LET HER CHOOSE 2 TACOS FROM THE 59 CENT MENU. SINCE THEN, SHE HAS BEEN TACO BELL OBSESSED. SHE GREW UP MOSTLY IN CALIFORNIA AND TEXAS, SO SHE KNOWS TACO BELL IS NOT REALLY MEXICAN FOOD, BUT SHE LOVES IT THE WAY PEOPLE LOVE THEIR HIGH SCHOOL GARAGE BANDS. NOSTALGIA IS YUMMY. HEATHER'S POETRY, FICTION, ESSAYS, AND ART CAN BE FOUND IN A VARIETY OF JOURNALS INCLUDING *THE AMERICAN POETRY REVIEW, PATERSON LITERARY REVIEW, RAGAZINE, THE KENTUCKY REVIEW,* AND MORE. SHE EARNED HER PH.D. IN ENGLISH CREATIVE WRITING FROM SUNY BINGHAMTON WHERE SHE IS A LECTURER. SHE IS ALSO THE EDITOR-IN-CHIEF FOR *BINGHAMTON WRITES,* A FIRST YEAR WRITING TEXTBOOK. AFTER WORK SHE GOES HOME TO WATCH TRUE CRIME. HER DOG, APPLE, BARKS AT SOMETHING INVISIBLE. HER CAT, FRANK, STANDS IN FRONT OF THE SCREEN POSING AND BLOCKING HER VIEW BECAUSE HE IS A MODEL. ON THE WEEKENDS, SHE WISHES SHE HAD A WASHING MACHINE.

SPECIAL THANKS

Special thanks to the many people who helped bring this book to life. Firstly, thanks to Michele McDannold who enthusiastically worked with me. She made the process easy and made me feel my work was valued. Michele is a gem. Thanks to the writers who have worked with me and encouraged me in the years I wrote and edited this book. To Misty Lassiter, who was with me in the early years when I was finding my voice. You were there through my bad poetry, bad heart, and hospital stay fashion shows; you were there when so many others ran away, during my surgery and recovery, and our fried scream potato after parties. I will never love a traffic cone like I loved ours. Thank you for being you with me. You are the Gilbert to my Gubar. To Heather Humphrey, the best Heather who ever Heathered, thank you for your support through so many tumultuous life changes, for teaching me how to adult, for not judging me when I'm not adult, for understanding my quirks, and for adjusting to them. You are so hardworking, brilliant, and plain fun, I feel honored that you are my friend. To Sarah Jefferis, a gifted poet and close pal, thank you for teaching me how to slice through what is unnecessary to get to the bones of my writing. You have helped me make my writing tighter and taught me about arrangements and subtext. Whether we are laughing over dominoes or writing for hours in Denny's, I always count our time as precious. To Wendy Stewart, a wonderful professor, mentor, and writer. Thank you for being so witty, wry, and paradoxically sincere. We all contain multitudes but I often think you have a galaxy behind your pupils, and the human eye can only focus on one planet at a time. Too bad for us. I am lucky to have you as a colleague and friend, even when you won't let me break into your house in my dreams. To Abby Murray, the kindest person I know. Your poems blow me away and your apple butter is gold. I feel so fortunate for the time we worked and taught together. You taught me that "no" is a complete sentence and how to deal with conflict productively. I still don't know who was supposed to be the mother and who was supposed to be the daughter the day that man accused us of this relationship, but you for sure had the wisdom. To Angela Runciman, my conference reading partner, conference planning co-chair, colleague and mate (Australian for you). I'm forever laughing when we get together. I'm glad we decided to finish our degrees instead of sell used watches to Boscovs but if things get dicey we know we have something to fall back on. Okay Man will forever be linked to you and I wish for Mariska Hargitay to bless you. To Virginia Shank, my bar hopping gal pal from my wilder days. I miss seeing your face, reading your gut punch poems, dancing in Merlin's, hearing your beautiful karaoke voice, when your boots were made for walking, and drinking miso soup in your hot apartment above Crepe Heaven to ward off hangovers. You have helped me tremendously professionally and personally. I don't deserve your generosity and general awesomeness. To Kristi Murray Costello, who I used to refer to as my more put together self. Something about us just clicked, which I imagine must happen a great deal with you. I never wanted to stop talking when we got together and one hour would just turn into five. Our ideas never ended and I know many of the poems I wrote during this period were at least in part because of you. You are socially gifted, academically gifted, and a wonderful writer too. We will also always have Big Brother. To the participants of Sappho's Circle, thank you for giving me feedback and a space to write. Thanks to my dissertation director Maria Mazziotti Gillan for encouraging me to write poetry that is real, raw, and unpretentious. Thanks to the late Robb Jackson for teaching me 90% of what I know about poetry and for valuing my voice. I also learned 90% of what I know about teaching from him. Finally, thanks to my partner Travis Pelkie. One summer I got mad at him and wrote a poem about how wrong he was. He sat in the audience while I read it to a crowd, then clapped at the end, smiling. This is the kind of partner every writer needs.

ACKNOWLEDGEMENTS

"20 Goals" Slink Chunk Press, October 2016

"Twenty Year Vows" *Kentucky Review*, 2016

"Parent & Child Development," published as: "Parent & Child Development 101" *Red Paint Hill Poetry Journal*, January 2016

"So much depends" Slink Chunk Press, December 2015

"How To Be a Woman in a Man's Idea" Slink Chunk Press, December 2015

"Imprinting" *Ragazine*, November 2015

"Rituals" *Ragazine*, November 2015

"Bugs on a Window in Arkansas" *Not One of Us #54*, September 2015

"The Happy Genius of My Household" *Eunoia Review* September 7, 2015

"Feral" *Eunoia Review*, September 4, 2015

"How to Read," published as: "My Soul" Slink Chunk Press, August 2015 "How To Fall in Love With a Straight Woman" Slink Chunk Press, August 2015

"13 Ways of Looking at My Mother" *Paterson Literary Review #43*, 2015

"So You Will Know Me" *Metonym* Volume V., Spring 2015

"How to Name Your Daughter" *Digging Through the Fat, Ripping Out the Heart*, March 2015

"How to Be Manic," "What Type of Person Are You?: Take the Quiz!" *Barking Sycamores #4*

"Proofing" *Festival Writer*, November 2014

"Ballerinas Don't Eat Cheezits," "How to Get an A," "Thanks to the Gideons," "Selfie #4," "Selfie #9," *Too Much: Tales of Excess*, anthology, Unknown Press, 2014: 165 - 192.

"Cicadas" *Uno Kudo 3*, 2013; *This is Poetry, Volume I: Women of the Small Press*, anthology, Citizens for Decent Literature Press. 2014: 28.

"Scared of the Dark" *This is Poetry, Volume I: Women of the Small Press*, anthology, Citizens for Decent Literature Press. 2014: 31.

"Heather Wants to Invest $40,000" *Kleft Jaw*, Issue #6, July 2014

"How to Make Ends Meet" *RedFez.* Issue 59. August 2013

"Chicken Tacos" *Red Fez* Volume 55, April 2013

"I Always Drive Over Potholes" *Citizens for Decent Literature*, April 2013

"How To Cook in a Coffee Pot" *Citizens for Decent Literature*, Issue #6, March 17, 2013

"D.A.R.E." *Citizens for Decent Literature*, Issue #6, March 17, 2013

"He said something about Hemingway" *Uno Kudo: Volume 2, Naked*, November 19, 2012

www.ingramcontent.com/pod-product-compliance
Lightning Source LLC
Chambersburg PA
CBHW020317130626
46549CB00003B/901